For Jamie

For information about permission to reproduce
selections from this book, write to Permissions,
Houghton Mifflin Harcourt Publishing Company,
215 Park Avenue South, New York,
New York 10003.

Houghton Mifflin Books for Children is an
imprint of Houghton Mifflin Harcourt
Publishing Company.

www.hmhbooks.com

The illustrations are torn- and cut-paper collage.

Library of Congress Cataloging-in-Publication
Data

Jenkins, Steve, 1952–
The beetle book / Steve Jenkins.
p. cm.
ISBN 978-0-547-68084-2
1. Beetles—Juvenile literature. I. Title.
QL576.2.J46 2011
595.76—dc23
2011027129

Manufactured in China
SCP 10 9 8 7 6 5 4 3 2
4500393232

Beetle variations

Beetles are found in an amazing range of shapes, sizes, and colors, but they all share the same basic design.

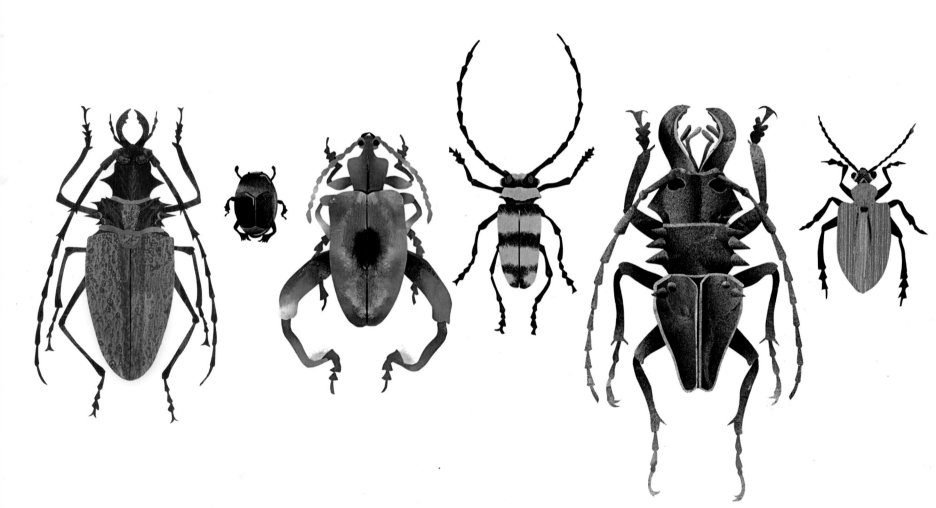

longhorn beetle   clown beetle   frog beetle   Asian longhorn beetle   giant longhorn beetle   lily beetle

Line up every kind of plant and animal
on Earth . . .

. . . and one of every four will be a beetle.

above and right: longhorn beetle
previous page: stag beetle

The
Beetle Book
by Steve Jenkins

Houghton Mifflin Books for Children • Houghton Mifflin Harcourt • Boston • New York

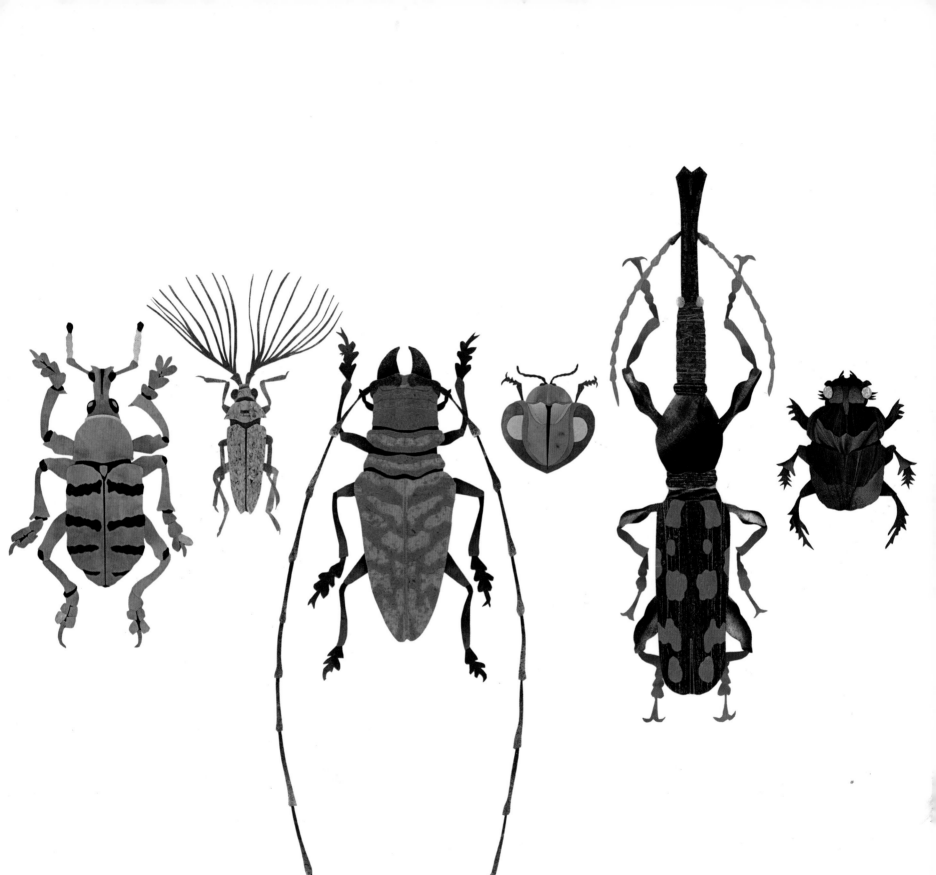

metallic green weevil   cedar beetle   flat-faced longhorn beetle   leaf beetle   Indonesian beetle   dung beetle

What is a beetle?

Beetles are insects. Like all insects, they have a pair of antennae, six legs, and three main body parts. This flower beetle is shown twice life-size.

Except for the oceans and polar regions, beetles are found in almost every habitat: grasslands, forests, jungles, lakes and rivers — even deserts.

More than 350,000 different kinds of beetle have been named. Thousands more are discovered every year. Altogether, there are probably more than a million beetle species.

Beetles sense their surroundings with eyes, ears, and antennae. Tiny hairs on the legs and body of many beetles can also detect sounds and odors.

A beetle's body is enclosed in a rigid shell called an exoskeleton. This hard casing provides support and protection.

A person who studies beetles is a **coleopterist** (co-lee-op-ter-ist).

Beetles evolved about 230 million years ago — around the same time as the dinosaurs.

Beetles don't have lungs or gills. Instead, they breathe through small openings on their body.

Beetle bits

All beetles are constructed on the same basic blueprint. There are a few exceptions, such as flightless ground beetles or eyeless cave beetles. Most beetles, however, have all of the parts described here.

Mandibles
Beetles use their mandibles, or jaws, to eat. Some beetles also use them to fight.

Mouth parts
The beetle's diet determines the shape of its mouth parts.

Antennae
These sensitive appendages are organs of smell and touch.

Head
The eyes, ears, mandibles, antennae, and brain are located here.

Eyes
Most beetles have compound eyes made up of many separate lenses, or facets.

Wing casings
Hardened outer wings protect the delicate inner wings. They swing out of the way when the beetle takes flight.

Thorax
The legs and wings attach to this part of the beetle's body.

Flight wings
The inner wings are thin and flexible. They fold up and tuck under the wing casings when not in use.

Abdomen
Food is digested here. The beetle's reproductive organs are also located in the abdomen.

Legs
Most beetles have four leg parts connected with joints that allow movement.

What's special about a beetle?

A few adaptations have helped beetles thrive in many different environments.

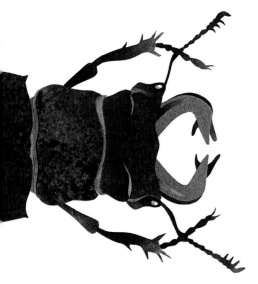

Beetles' mandibles, or jaws, come in a variety of shapes and sizes, which allows different kinds of beetles to eat a wide variety of food. The jaws above belong to a **stag beetle,** shown two times life-size.

tortoise beetle   rose chafer beetle

(Silhouettes throughout the book are actual size.)

Perhaps the innovation that has been most helpful to the beetle is its pair of rigid outer wings. This armored covering, shown here on a **rose chafer beetle,** protects the insect from predators and other dangers.

The **mottled tortoise beetle** uses its oversize wing casings like a turtle's shell, tucking its head and legs underneath when danger threatens.

This **jewel beetle,** shown five times life-size, swings its wing covers out of the way to take flight. Being able to fly helps the beetle escape danger, find food, or locate a mate.

Beetle senses

Beetles sense their surroundings with their eyes, ears, and antennae. And some beetles have other, more unusual sensory organs.

The **forest fire beetle** has special heat-sensing spots on its body. It can detect a fire from more than 20 miles (32 kilometers) away. These beetles fly to the site of a forest fire and lay their eggs in charred wood — wood that is now free of predators.

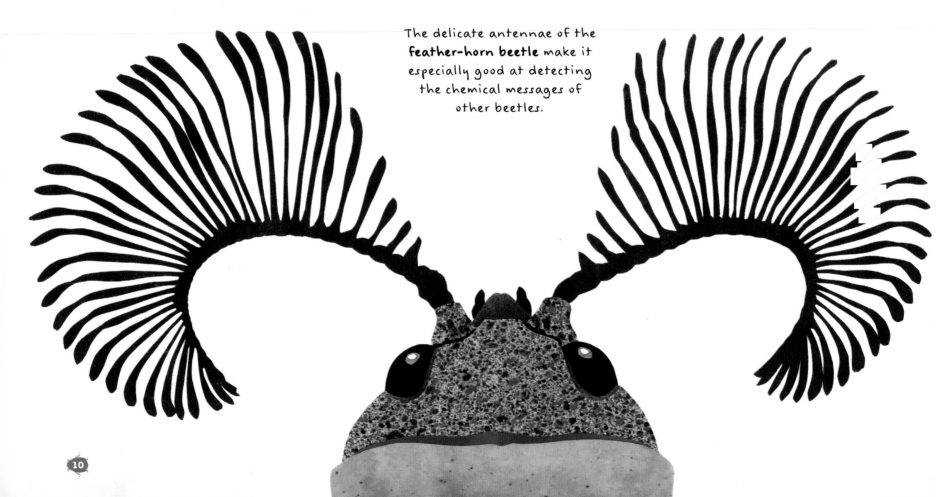

The delicate antennae of the **feather-horn beetle** make it especially good at detecting the chemical messages of other beetles.

Tufts of hair on the body of the **African jewel beetle** are sensitive to vibration. They help the beetle avoid predators.

Like most beetles, the **Japanese beetle** has compound eyes. This kind of eye lets the beetle see a lot of its surroundings. Unlike human eyes, compound eyes can follow moving objects without moving themselves.

The **whirligig beetle** skims along the surface of ponds and rivers. Whirligigs have four eyes — two look above the water and two peer below the surface.

The **sugarcane beetle,** which is active at night, can hear sounds that are too high-pitched for humans to detect. When this beetle hears the squeaks of a bat, it flies erratically to avoid being eaten.

forest fire beetle

feather-horn beetle

African jewel beetle

Japanese beetle

whirligig beetle

sugarcane beetle

Battling beetles

Males of some beetle species fight with each other to win a mate. Many of these beetles use impressive horns, jaws, or legs in combat.

This **stag beetle,** shown at life-size, uses its huge jaws to spar with other males. They look dangerous, but these jaws aren't strong enough to break a human's skin.

The **long-armed chafer beetle** and the smaller **cape stag beetle,** at left, are both shown at two times life-size. The chafer fights with his armored front legs. The cape stag beetle slides its wedge-shaped jaws under an opponent and flips it onto its back. These beetles fight males of their own kind, not each other.

These **rhinoceros beetles,** shown twice life-size, are dueling on a branch high in a tree. The loser will be tossed from its perch and probably miss out on its chance to mate with the female waiting nearby.

Growing up

Most beetles pass through four life stages: egg, larva, pupa, and adult. The entire cycle can take just a few months or as long as thirty years.

In the spring, a female **ladybird beetle** — also known as a ladybug — lays her eggs on a leaf. About four days later, ladybird larvae crawl from their eggs and begin to feed on aphids and other small insects.

The larvae have enormous appetites and grow quickly. A ladybird larva goes through four stages, shedding its skin and getting larger each time. It spends about three months as a larva.

Some beetle larvae go through only one stage; others, as many as thirty. Finally, the larva stops eating and becomes a pupa.

The larva of a **Hercules beetle,** shown life-size, feeds on rotting plant material. These juicy larvae — and those of many other beetles — are eaten by people in some parts of the world.

ladybird beetle

burying beetle

metallic wood-boring beetle

giraffe weevil

Burying beetles are one of the few insects that take care of their young. The mother lays her eggs on a dead animal, then both parents work together to bury it. The parents guard the eggs, then clean and protect the larvae, which will feed on the dead animal.

After about a week, the pupa splits open and an adult beetle emerges. It will feed for a few weeks, then find a spot to spend the winter. In the spring it will awaken, look for a mate, and start the cycle over again.

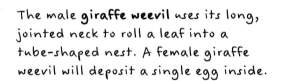

The male **giraffe weevil** uses its long, jointed neck to roll a leaf into a tube-shaped nest. A female giraffe weevil will deposit a single egg inside.

The **metallic wood-boring beetle** lays its eggs in dry wood. The adult beetles may not emerge until thirty years later.

Plant eaters

Most beetles are vegetarians. Beetles of one kind or another will consume every part of a plant, including leaves, bark, roots, sap, and flower pollen. Other beetles eat fungus or dung.

The **thick-legged flower beetle** feeds on pollen. Like a honeybee, it is a pollinator, helping plants reproduce by carrying pollen from one flower to another.

Without **dung beetles,** the world's grasslands would soon be buried in animal droppings. This beetle is rolling a ball of dung back to its burrow to provide food for its mate and its offspring.

thick-legged
flower beetle

dung beetle

pleasing
fungus beetle

boll weevil

Colorado potato
beetle

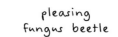

The **pleasing fungus beetle** makes a meal of mushrooms and other fungi — a food source that is overlooked by many animals.

Sipping plant juices with its long snout, the **boll weevil** attacks the flowers and fruit of the cotton plant. It is a pest, causing serious damage to cotton crops.

The **Colorado potato beetle** is also a pest. It eats the leaves of potato and tomato plants, weakening or killing them.

Hunters and scavengers

Some beetles are hunters, catching and eating worms, spiders, insects, and — in a few cases — small fish and amphibians. Other beetles eat insect larvae or feed on dead animals.

The **hide beetle** eats the dried skin and flesh of dead animals. Natural history museums use these beetles to clean animal bones for display.

The **ladybird beetle** is a predator with a big appetite. In one day a single ladybug can consume hundreds of aphids — tiny insects that suck plant juices. Gardeners use ladybugs to help get rid of aphids.

The **rove beetle** hunts insects, spiders, and snails. It shoots a long rod tipped with a bristly pad from its mouth. This sticky pad attaches to the beetle's prey. The body of this beetle contains a toxin that is more potent than cobra venom, protecting it from larger predators.

ladybird beetle

rove beetle

hide beetle

six-spotted green tiger beetle

The fierce **six-spotted green tiger beetle** hunts by sight. It stalks its prey, runs it down, and tears it to pieces with its razor-sharp jaws. Tiger beetles eat spiders, worms, and other insects.

Let's talk

Hissing, chirping, thumping, and squeaking: many beetles and other insects make sounds. And a few have an ability that is common among deep-sea creatures but unusual on land: they can light up.

The **tok-tokkie,** pictured twice life-size, signals its mate by thumping its abdomen loudly against the ground.

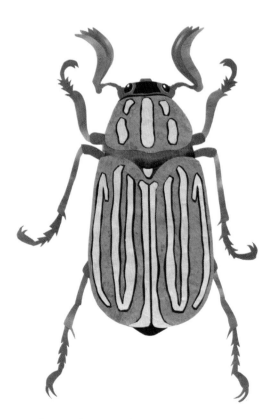

The **Fijian long-horn beetle,** shown actual size, makes a loud hissing noise by squeezing air from beneath its wing covers.

When it's disturbed or picked up, the **ten-lined June beetle** produces a startling sound that has been described as a raspy squeak. This beetle is shown three times life size.

The **firefly** creates its glow — called bioluminescence — by mixing two chemicals in a special chamber in its abdomen. Male fireflies signal females by flashing their light on and off in a precise pattern. The females reply with their own sequence of flashes.

Some fireflies use their light in a different way. A female imitates the flashes of a male firefly of a different species. When the male answers and approaches her, she devours him.

Tap tap. Tap tap. It's a **deathwatch beetle,** knocking its head against the sides of its wooden burrow to signal a mate. When these beetle bore into the walls of a house, their taps are loud enough for us to hear.

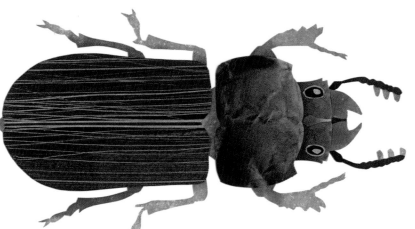

Disturb a **peg beetle** and it makes a loud squeaking sound by rubbing its wings against its abdomen. It may be alerting other peg bugs to danger.

firefly

peg beetle

deathwatch
beetle

Chemical warfare

Beetles have developed quite an arsenal of chemical weapons. They defend themselves with poison, foul-tasting fluids, or jets of boiling hot liquid. The bright colors of many of these beetles warn predators that they are **not** good to eat.

The brilliant color of this **true weevil** is saying, "I taste terrible."

The body of this **leaf beetle** is poisonous. But it has another trick up its sleeve. It produces a substance that is extremely sticky. If an ant tries to eat one these beetles, it will discover that its jaws are glued together.

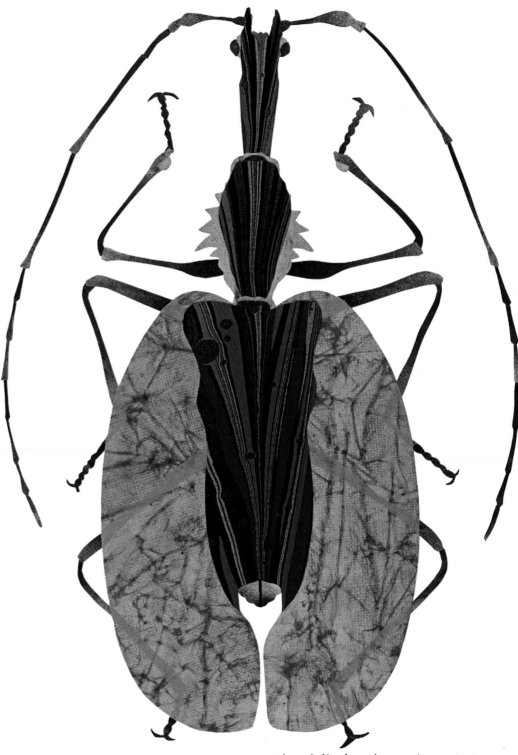

The **violin beetle** repels predators by squirting acid from a gland in its abdomen. Those who handle this insect risk getting a painful burn on their fingers.

The **bombardier beetle** has one of the most impressive beetle defenses. It squirts a blinding, boiling hot liquid into the face of an attacker. The chemical explosion powering this spray makes a loud popping sound.

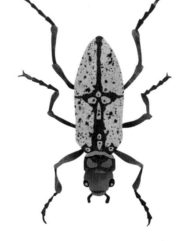

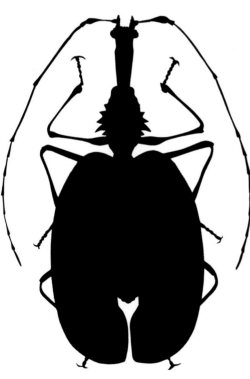

The toxin from a **iron cross blister beetle** produces painful blisters on human skin. These beetles are dangerous — a horse can die from accidentally swallowing a few with its feed.

The **stink beetle** defends itself with a discharge of foul-smelling liquid.

violin beetle

true weevil

leaf beetle

bombardier beetle

iron cross blister beetle

stink beetle

Clever disguises

Some beetles discourage predators by imitating bees or wasps — insects with painful stings. Others fool ants or termites into caring for them and giving them food. There is even a beetle that disguises itself as a pile of bird poop.

When the **ironclad beetle** is threatened, it pulls in its legs and holds very still. Now it appears to be nothing but a pile of bird droppings.

The two large eye spots of the **eyed click beetle** fool predators into mistaking this insect for a larger animal.

The **ant beetle** looks and smells like an ant. The fierce army ants it lives among are fooled. They think the beetle is one of them, and they feed and protect it.

The **golden spider beetle** is harmless, but it looks a lot like its poisonous, eight-legged distant relative. It's a good thing predators can't count!

The **wasp beetle** may be a harmless plant eater, but it looks like a wasp. It even flies like a wasp. If this beetle is lucky, predators will fear a painful sting and leave it alone.

ironclad
beetle

eyed click
beetle

ant
beetle

golden
spider beetle

wasp
beetle

A trick of the light

A shiny, fast-moving beetle glitters in the grass. Other beetles hide in plain sight, blending in with leaves and bark.

Many beetles are masters of camouflage. Their colors, shapes, and patterns keep them hidden from their enemies — or their prey.

bark-gnawing beetle

rose chafer beetle

metallic wood-boring beetle

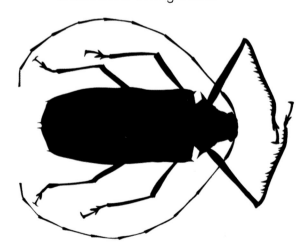

harlequin beetle

Despite its name, the **bark-gnawing beetle** feeds on insects, including other beetles. Its bright color would seem to be a disadvantage for a hunter. But as this beetle scurries along, its metallic shell flashes in the light and it seems to appear first in one place, then another.

As it clings to a leaf, this **rose chafer beetle** seems to be part of the plant.

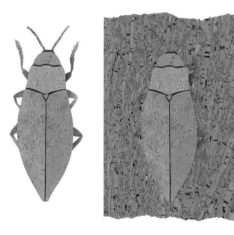

This **metallic wood-boring beetle** lives on rough tree bark. There its bumpy, splotchy body is almost invisible.

The **harlequin beetle** looks as if it would stand out in any crowd. But this beetle makes its home on colorful lichen-covered tree trunks, where its bold markings help it blend in.

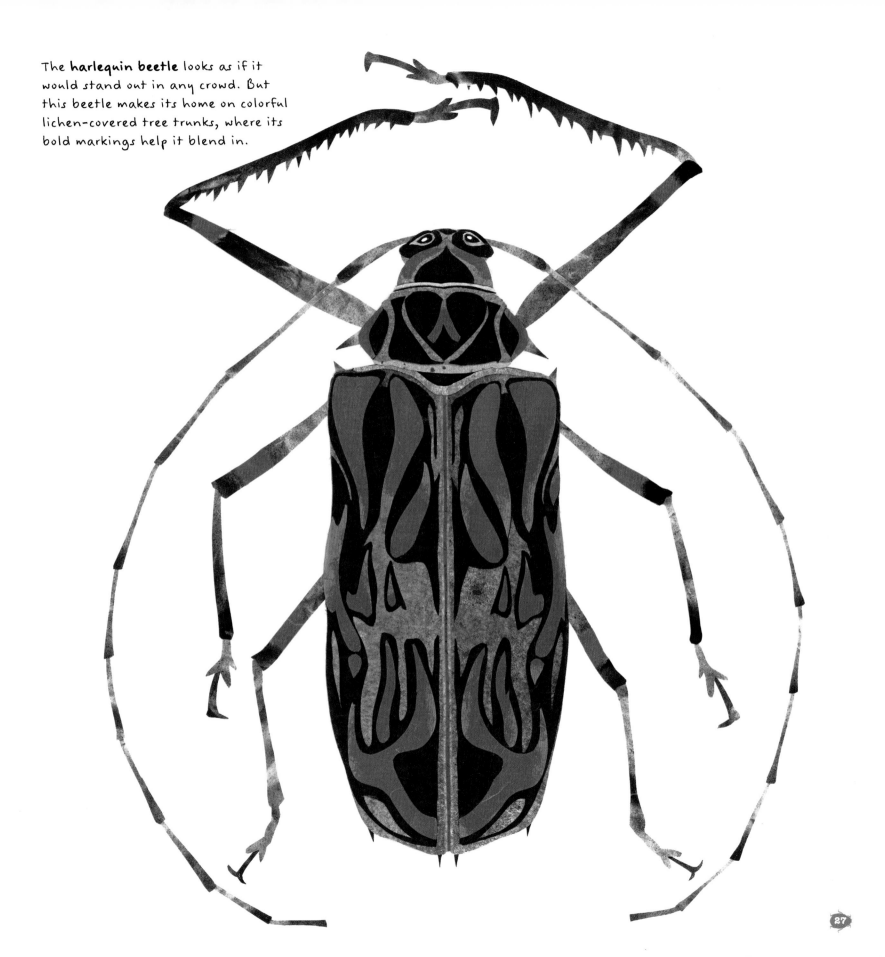

Move!

Running, crawling, flying, swimming, digging, or jumping — beetles get around in lots of different ways.

The **eggplant flea beetle** has powerful back legs, and can jump so quickly when disturbed that it seems to simply disappear.

The **Australian tiger beetle** is the fastest runner in the insect world. If a human could run as fast — for her size — as a tiger beetle, she'd be moving as fast as a jet airplane.

The tiny **stenus beetle** can walk on water. When it needs to move quickly, it releases a chemical that breaks the surface tension of the water behind it, propelling it at high speed across the surface.

eggplant
flea beetle

Australian tiger
beetle

stenus beetle

green June
beetle

diving beetle

mole beetle

click beetle

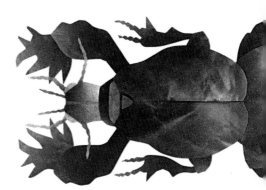

Despite its bulky appearance, the **green June beetle** is an accomplished flyer and a common sight as it buzzes around porch lights in warm weather.

The **diving beetle** spends its life in the water, using its back legs as paddles to swim on and under the water.

With shovel-like front legs, the **mole beetle** digs its way through the dirt.

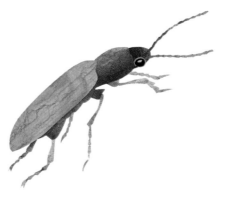

If it's threatened, the **click beetle** rolls onto its back, cocks a springlike mechanism on its abdomen, and flips high into the air. This sudden jump and the loud click sound it makes confuses the beetle's enemies.

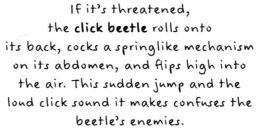

Beetles big and little

Some beetles are almost too small to see. Others — such as the ones shown here life-size — can be frighteningly large.

The dot inside the circle shows the size of the world's smallest beetle, the **clown beetle.**

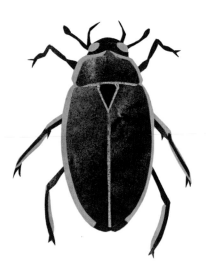

The **giant diving beetle** is big enough to catch and eat small fish and frogs.

The **African goliath beetle** is almost as big as a person's hand. This slow-moving, plant-eating insect is sometimes kept as a pet.

An Australian beetle, **Wallace's longicorn,** has the longest antennae of any insect.

The **titan beetle** is the world's longest beetle. Its jaws are powerful enough to snap a pencil in half. This huge insect lives in the Amazon rainforest.

Many beetles — such as the scarab beetle, the jewel beetle, and the lightning bug — have common names. But these names can be confusing. For example, there are more than 30,000 different kinds of scarab beetle, found all over the world. To be more precise, biologists give a Latin name to each individual species of plant or animal. To learn more about a particular beetle, it helps to know its scientific name. The list at right gives the Latin names for each beetle in this book, along with the part of the world where it is found. If a beetle's size is not shown in the book, its length is also listed here.

Bibliography

A Field Guide to the Beetles of North America.
By Richard E. White. Houghton Mifflin Company, 1983.

An Inordinate Fondness for Beetles.
By Arthur V. Evans and Charles L. Bellamy. University of California Press. 2000.

For Love of Insects.
By Thomas Eisner. The Belknap Press of Harvard University Press. 2003.

Guide to Observing Insect Lives.
By Donald Stokes. Little, Brown and Company. 1983.

Identifying Bugs and Beetles.
By Ken Preston-Mafham. Chartwell Books, Inc. 1997.

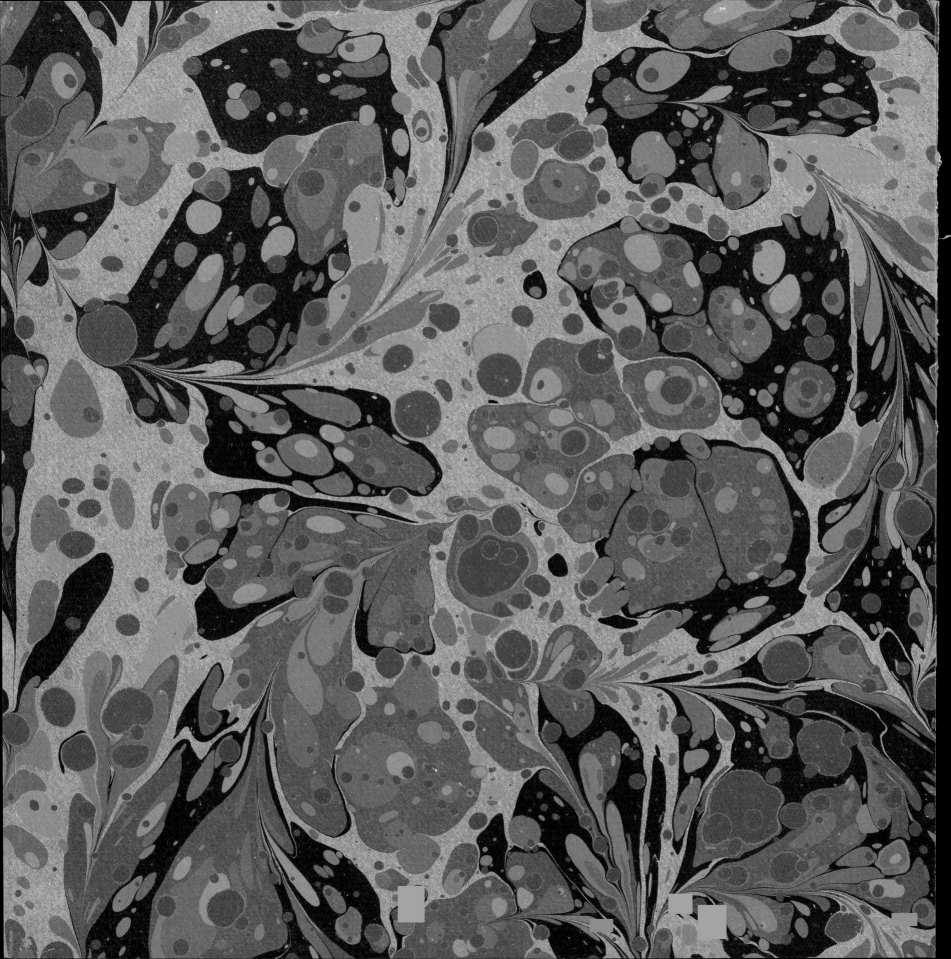